HOUGHTON-LE-SPRING
AND
HETTON-LE-HOLE
IN OLD PHOTOGRAPHS

THE OLD TOWN HALL and Covered Market, Newbottle Street, Houghton-le-Spring in around 1900.

HOUGHTON-LE-SPRING
AND
HETTON-LE-HOLE
IN OLD PHOTOGRAPHS

COLLECTED BY
KEN RICHARDSON

ALAN SUTTON
1989

Alan Sutton Publishing
Gloucester

First published 1989

British Library Cataloguing in Publication Data

Houghton-le-Spring and Hetton-le-Hole
in old photographs.
1. Tyne and Wear (Metropolitan county).
Sunderland. Hetton-le-Hole & Houghton-
le-Spring, history. Hetton-le-Hole, history.
Houghton-le-Spring, history
I. Richardson, Ken.
942.8'71

ISBN 0-86299-577-9

Front cover illustration: At the pawnshop, Smith's Terrace, Easington Lane in
around 1905.

Typesetting and origination by
Alan Sutton Publishing.
Printed in Great Britain by
Dotesios Printers Limited.

CONTENTS

LAMBTON BRICKWORKS at New Lambton in around 1937. Left to right: R. Avery, F. Rodgerson, J. Rodgerson.

INTRODUCTION

Houghton-le-Spring and Hetton-le-Hole are neighbouring small towns in north-east England, situated five miles from the North Sea coast and midway between the historic city of Durham and the port town of Sunderland. Both are now within the boundary of the Borough of Sunderland but formerly gave their names to sizeable Urban Districts and, until recently, were important centres of coal mining.

These twin towns, together with 18 associated villages form the subject of this book, which endeavours to portray, by means of old photographs, how the area looked in years past and to give glimpses of many aspects of life in the years between 1880 and the 1960s.

The large area which is now occupied by the Houghton and Hetton districts, and the now disparate villages of Bournmoor and West Rainton, was in earlier times all within the extensive rural parish of Houghton-le-Spring, one of the great holdings of the Prince Bishops of Durham. Then embracing some 18 townships and villages, this large parish extended from Bishopwearmouth, southwards to the boundary of the parish of St Giles and from Seaham westwards to Chester-le-Street, with the scenic River Wear forming the north-west boundary.

At the centre of this extensive parish lay the township of Houghton-le-Spring and the parish church of St Michael and All Angels, which still stands today having served the parish for almost a thousand years. Through the centuries there has been a long line of distinguished rectors at Houghton-le-Spring, some of whom subsequently attained high office in the Church of England, including two who became Archbishops of Canterbury; William Sancroft (rector 1661–1664) and Thomas Secker (rector 1723–1727). However, the most remarkable of all Houghton rectors was Bernard Gilpin, who was appointed rector in 1557 and remained at Houghton until his death in 1584. Known even to this day as the 'Apostle of the North' and 'Father of the Poor', he devoted his life to the care of the people of his extensive parish.

Like the rest of rural England the large parish of Houghton-le-Spring consisted of small rural communities with an economy based on agriculture. By the late seventeenth century, however, this rural way of life was undergoing great change. Villagers were losing their landholding as the open fields were being enclosed and there was growing evidence that rich coal seams lay beneath this pastoral landscape. It was the exploitation of this mineral wealth, by landowners and entrepreneurs during the eighteenth and nineteenth centuries, that led to the growth of the Houghton and Hetton district.

As early as the fourteenth century coal had been mined on a small scale to the west and north-west of Houghton at places such as Biddick, Finchale, Lumley and Rainton where coal occurred near the surface, or was exposed at the banks of the River Wear. By the early eighteenth century, coal was being transported several miles overland by horse-drawn waggons along wooden waggon ways from the various collieries to the river side at South Biddick. Here the coal was loaded into keel-boats, which were then navigated down the River Wear to the port of Sunderland and the waiting sailing ships bound for London and the continent.

The demand for coal increased rapidly during the first half of the nineteenth century to meet the ever-growing demands of the 'steam age'. North-eastern coal, including that from Houghton and Hetton, was required in ever-increasing quantities to fuel the nation's ironworks and the hungry furnaces of the steam driven machinery of Victorian industry. Many collieries were opened in the area during this period and vast amounts of coal were exported from the River Wear and the port of Sunderland. Other industries were established alongside the collieries; cokeworks, gasworks, iron foundries, brickyards, potteries and engineering workshops. From the colliery waggon ways the early railways were developed to move coal more efficiently from the collieries to the ports.

The collieries and other industries created a great deal of employment, thus large numbers of workers with their families were attracted to the area from other parts of the country, seeking work, wages and living accommodation. The population of the entire parish of Houghton-le-Spring in 1801 was only 6,414. By the year 1851 the population of the same area – by then divided into several parishes – had increased to 20,260 and, by 1891, had risen to 45,700. During this period many rows of miners' houses were built by the colliery companies for the increasing number of employees and several new settlements were established.

With the growing population, many new churches, chapels, schools and meeting halls were built. Between the years 1838 and 1913, the original parish of Houghton-le-Spring was divided into no less than 11 new parishes as detailed here:

Penshaw	1838	West Rainton	1838
Hetton-le-Hole	1847	East Rainton	1866
Bournmoor	1866	Easington Lane	1869
Chilton Moor	1872	Eppleton	1883
Herrington	1884	Newbottle	1886
Shiney Row	1913.		

The picturesque town of Houghton-le-Spring stands at the base of a range of limestone hills which shelter the town from the north and east. It is also situated on the Durham–Sunderland highway at a point where it is intersected by several other important routes.

Houghton-le-Spring derives its name from the attractive hills which overlook the town and the many mineral water springs that formerly flowed from the limestone rock. The name 'Houghton' is derived from two Old English words 'Hough' (Hoc) and 'Ton' (Tun) which together as 'Houghton' (Hocton) mean 'homestead or settlement on the spur of a hill'. There are several versions of the derivation of the second element 'le-Spring', but the most likely is that it originated from the abundance of fresh water springs which formerly existed at Houghton, so that the name became Houghton-in-the-Springs and later Houghton-le-Spring.

To the east of Houghton town centre lies the old Market Place, tastefully redeveloped in the 1950s. It was here that the original Saxon village was established with cottages and farmsteads skirting the village green, through which the clear waters of the Houghton Burn flowed.

There is also evidence that the Houghton area was inhabited long before Saxon times. On the higher ground to the south-east of Houghton-le-Spring, near to the summit of Copt Hill, is a prominent mound surmounted by a group of sentinel-like trees known as the 'Seven Sisters'. This landscape feature is an ancient burial 'barrow' which, when excavated in 1877, revealed cremated remains from the Neolithic period (later Stone Age) and of secondary burials of later date, together with a cinerary urn now in the keeping of the British Museum.

Coal mining came relatively late into the township of Houghton-le-Spring with Houghton colliery being sunk between 1823 and 1827. Eventually it was to become one of the largest mines in the area and, at its peak in the early twentieth century, provided employment for over 2,000 men and boys. Throughout the nineteenth century Houghton township experienced continuous growth; in 1801 the population was only 996, by 1841 it had increased to 3,433 and by 1901 the population had risen to 7,858.

Houghton township became the main shopping and commercial centre for the mining communities of the district, with a great variety of shops and business premises. The local Board of Health was formed in 1854 and the Houghton Urban District was created in 1894.

Hetton-le-Hole, lying to the immediate south of Houghton-le-Spring, stands on the A182 Houghton–Easington Road. Although Hetton has a history reaching back for almost a thousand years it remained a small village within the parish of Houghton-le-Spring until the opening of the Hetton collieries in the 1820s.

The name of Hetton-le-Hole is derived from two Old English words 'Heppe' and 'Dune' which together as 'Heppedune' denoted Bramble Hill. Later dialect forms were variously given as 'Hepedon', 'Hepdon' and 'Hepton'. The name was adopted by the local land-owning family, the De-Heptons, who owned the manor of Hepdon from the earliest times. This early manorial residence seems to have been located at Heppedune (the Bramble Hill) identified with Hetton-on-the-Hill near Elemore. At some later date a new manor house was built in a more sheltered position in the valley, near to where the village of Hetton-le-Hole became established. In a rebuilt form, this house became known as Hetton Hall and it stood until 1923 on a site near the present leisure centre and sports ground at Hetton Park.

Through the centuries the Hetton estate was held by many different owners, including the Musgrave and Spearman families. In 1746 the estate was purchased by the Countess Dowager of Strathmore who gave it to her son, the Honourable Thomas Lyon, whose family lived at Hetton Hall until 1812. The estate finally passed to the late Honourable Frances Bowes-Lyon, a relative of the Queen Mother. Hetton Hall remained unoccupied after 1812 for many years until the eminent mining engineer, Nicholas Wood, came to reside there, although the estate was still owned by the Bowes-Lyon family. After Nicholas Wood died in 1865 the Hall was only occasionally used by the Bowes-Lyon family and it was finally demolished in the early 1920s.

The undulating landscape that lies to the east of Houghton and Hetton consists of a thick bed of magnesian limestone and until the early nineteenth century it was a matter of conjecture as to whether coal existed under this limestone. An unsuccessful attempt to sink a mine shaft was made by John Lyon Esq. in 1815, to the west of Hetton woods. The Hetton Coal Company was formed in 1819 and commenced the sinking of the Hetton Lyons Colliery in December 1820, with coal production starting in November 1822. This colliery was the first to be successfully sunk through the water-bearing magnesian limestone, which at this point was 156ft thick and underlain by a bed of sand 4ft 4ins thick.

Coal from the Hetton Colliery was transported by the Hetton Colliery Railway a distance of some eight miles to the port of Sunderland. Engineered by George Stephenson, one of the world's earliest railways was opened on 18 November 1822. Traversing the high ground of Copt Hill and Warden Law, it utilized a combination of stationary engines, self-acting inclines and locomotives. The railway was to continue successfully until its closure in 1959.

The successful winning of Hetton Colliery was a significant breakthrough in mining technology and heralded a new era in the development of the East Durham Coalfield. Following on the success of the Hetton enterprise, other collieries were successfully won through the water-bearing strata, although in some instances this was not without a great deal of difficulty and financial expenditure. Collieries that opened in the locality during this period were Houghton (1823–1827), Eppleton (1825–1833), Elemore (1824–1827), South Hetton (1831–1832) and Murton (1838–1843).

The small village of Hetton-le-Hole expanded rapidly, with many rows of colliery houses being built at Eppleton, Hetton and Easington Lane. In the year 1801 the population of Hetton was only 212 but with the expansion of the collieries the population had, by 1851, increased to 5,664. A small Anglican church was erected at Hetton in 1832 as a chapel of ease to Houghton. In 1847 this became the parish church, when the parish of Hetton-le-Hole was formed from that of Houghton. This small church was to serve Hetton and its people very well until it was dismantled in 1898–1901 and replaced by the present church of St Nicholas, this being consecrated by the Bishop of Durham on 29 April 1901.

As the nineteenth century advanced the township continued to progress with a great variety of shops and business premises being established, not only at central Hetton but also at Eppleton and Easington Lane. The Parish of Hetton was later subdivided with the creation of two daughter parishes, that of Easington Lane in 1869 and that of Eppleton in 1883. In 1895 the Hetton Urban District was formed, which then consisted of Hetton, Eppleton and Easington Lane, with the wards of Moorsley and Rainton being added in 1937.

In the 1930s both Houghton and Hetton Urban District Councils introduced redevelopment programmes, replacing older dwellings with pleasant new housing estates and these revitalization programmes were sustained well into the post-war years. The demand for coal continued into the mid-twentieth century but, by the 1960s, coal reserves were nearing exhaustion and the local mining industry was in decline. Houghton Colliery closed in 1981, while Eppleton, the last of the Hetton collieries, merged with Murton in 1986, thus bringing to a close an era that had endured for over 150 years.

The area has experienced tremendous changes in recent years, the local mining industry is no longer the dominant force that it once was. Many colliery sites have been reclaimed to provide pleasant landscaped areas and modern industrial estates that now attract alternative industries. Houghton and Hetton are now modern and progressive towns with attractive residential, commercial and shopping facilities and, although an area with a rich heritage, it moves proudly into an exciting new age.

SECTION ONE

Houghton-le-Spring

DURHAM ROAD AND BROADWAY in the early 1930s, at that time a busy thoroughfare with several bus stops. The range of shops and offices seen at the right of the photograph had then recently been converted from buildings of the former Robinson's brewery which closed in 1925.

HOUGHTON CROSSROADS in the 1930s, many years before the town centre was by-passed by the modern road system. At that time this was a busy junction with a policeman on point duty. In the background are Houghton Parish Church and War Memorial.

THE PARISH CHURCH of St Michael and All Angels in the 1930s. It is probable that a church has stood on this site from Saxon times. Most of the present structure dates from the thirteenth and fourteenth centuries, while the tower dates from 1824 and replaced an earlier lead-covered steeple.

HOUGHTON RECTORY AND GROUNDS with the parish church in the background, in around 1890. Standing to the left of the photograph is the Hon. John Grey (Rector 1847–1895) with Mrs Grey and in the centre is Alice Hamilton, their lady gardener.

HOUGHTON KEPIER GRAMMAR SCHOOL in around 1905. This was founded in 1574 by Rector Bernard Gilpin. He was generously supported in the venture by John Heath, who endowed the school with the income of the dissolved Kepier hospital, near Durham City, from which the name is taken. Although the school closed in 1922, the building continues to serve the community as Kepier Hall.

HOUGHTON CHURCH LADS' BRIGADE at Kepier Hall in 1934. At the centre of the group is the Revd R. Watson, Rector of Houghton, with assistant clergy.

TRAMCARS of the Sunderland District Electric Tramways at Houghton Broadway, in around 1918. This tramway service started in 1905 and the system closed down in 1925. The route ran from Easington Lane to Grangetown via Hetton, Houghton, Newbottle and the Herringtons, with branch lines to both Fence Houses and Penshaw railway stations.

A VIEW OF BROADWAY in around 1895 with the White Lion hotel at the centre. To the left, Newbottle Street and, to the right, Sunderland Street with the Golden Lion Inn at the far right of the photograph.

IN FORMER TIMES houses were illuminated by oil lamps, with the paraffin oil being delivered by horse and cart. This photograph of around 1895 features such an oil cart with the proprietors, Mr and Mrs Hamilton, outside their home at Vine Place, Houghton.

THE ROYAL OAK INN, Newbottle Street, in the 1920s. This was demolished in the early 1930s and was replaced in 1935 by the Jubilee buildings which included Moore's grocery store and Jaconelli's ice-cream parlour. Woolworth's stores now stands on this site.

AN EARLY VIEW OF NEWBOTTLE STREET, in around 1906, with Houghton colliery visible in the background. It is interesting to note that, until 1908, buildings did not exist at the west side of the street.

NEWBOTTLE STREET, looking north in around 1914. At the extreme left of the photograph is the New Gaiety Theatre, rebuilt as the Grand Theatre in 1930 and now the site of Gateway supermarket. Next door to the Gaiety is the Empire Theatre, which still survives as a Bingo Hall.

NEWBOTTLE STREET, looking south in 1912. Although the owners and functions of the many shops in this busy thoroughfare have changed since the days of the photograph, the layout and character of the street remains much the same today.

RIANI'S ICE-CREAM PARLOUR AND CONFECTIONER'S SHOP, Newbottle Street, in around 1920 with Mr Columbo Riani, proprietor, standing in the doorway. The Riani family still run a popular ice-cream parlour and snack bar from these same premises today.

NEWBOTTLE STREET, with the corner premises of Mr W. Greenhow, glass, china and hardware merchant, in around the year 1905. This family firm, founded as long ago as 1805, is still trading today from these same premises.

THE NORTH END OF NEWBOTTLE STREET, looking north in the 1930s. At the extreme right, part of the premises of C.E. Tymns, draper, can be seen, while the large building towards the centre is the Lambton Arms, which still exists today.

HOUGHTON COLLIERY WELFARE HALL AND SPORTS PAVILION in the 1930s. The Hall was opened in 1931 while the extensive grounds opened earlier in 1925. Today the Hall forms part of a modern leisure and sports complex, which extends over the site of the former bowling greens, tennis courts and pavilion.

HOUGHTON COLLIERY WELFARE GROUNDS with gymnasium and bandstand, looking west in the 1930s. In recent times the site has been redeveloped as part of the leisure and sports complex.

HOUGHTON COLLIERY WELFARE BOWLING CLUB in the 1930s.

HOUGHTON COLLIERY WELFARE AFC, winners of the Houghton Aged Miners' Cup and Houghton League Challenge Cup. Season 1931–1932. Back row: R. Wardle, T. Newton, C. Naisbett, E. Margerham. Fourth row: A. Pearn, W. Wardle, T. Simpson, R. Patrick, R. Hall, G. Dixon, T. Hedley. Third row: J. Dixon, T. Dixon, A. Ashman, J. Smith, W. Brown, T. Coxon. Second row: J. Herron, T. Ball, G. Simpson, E. Atkinson, E. Burn, W. Atkinson, W. Fairhurst (Vice-President). Front row: J. Lidford, M. Dixon (Chairman), W. Stokoe (President), J. Gregory, W. Rodgerson (Vice President), W. Jacques (Secretary), B. Vickers.

HOUGHTON COUNCIL SCHOOL, Newbottle Street, opened in 1909 with separate departments for girls, boys and infants. The photograph features a group of young children outside the infants' department in the year 1919.

A GROUP OF SCHOOLBOYS outside the entrance of the boys' department, Houghton Council School in around 1925 with Mr S. Elliott, headmaster, at the left.

MOTOR CHARABANCS had become popular by the 1920s for organised day-outings to both the countryside and seaside resorts. The photograph shows Houghton folk sitting in a charabanc outside Stanger's butcher's shop at the bottom of Hopper Street in around 1920.

STEAM ROAD VEHICLES were in regular use for freight haulage until around 1930. The photograph features a Foden steam wagon belonging to the family firm of E. Metcalfe and Sons, haulage contractors, outside their Newbottle Street premises in the 1920s.

HOUGHTON COLLIERY AND GASWORKS in 1895. The colliery in the background of the photograph was completed in 1827 and, by 1920, provided employment for some 2,000 men and boys. Houghton gasworks in the foreground, opened in 1835.

THIS PHOTOGRAPH shows a group of miners at Houghton Colliery waiting to go underground in around 1920.

HOUGHTON COLLIERY AMBULANCE TEAM at Herrington Burn YMCA hut, 1936. Winners of the Lambton and Silksworth Collieries Silver Challenge Cup, 1936. Back row: G. Coulson, A. Marshall, J. Wardle, Mr E. Martin (Colliery Manager). Front row: T. Ellis, G. Saxon, T. Hedley.

ST MARK'S MISSION CHURCH, Quarry Row, in around 1930. Opened in 1883 with accommodation for 200 people, the Mission served the spiritual needs of the Quarry Row community under the authority of the Rector of Houghton-le-Spring. In the post-war years the building became part of the National Coal Board Mining Training Centre and it was demolished in around 1964.

THE MAIN NEWBOTTLE–HOUGHTON ROAD, looking towards Houghton. On the right side of the photograph is Quarry Row West; on the left side, Newbottle Row and two rows of Lambton Street. The area was cleared in the 1960s and today is pleasantly landscaped.

RAINE'S GENERAL DEALER'S SHOP, Quarry Row West, in around 1930. Kerr's garage now stands on this site.

THE LOWER END OF SUNDERLAND STREET, looking north-east, in the 1930s, when this was the main Durham–Sunderland road and a busy shopping thoroughfare. On the extreme right, Pallister's drapery store is now the site of the modern Broadway House DHSS offices. Beyond Pallister's stands Frederick Place and the entrance to the 'Lake' fairground.

THE BUTCHER'S SHOP OF MR ALF ORMSTON is shown in this photograph of around 1912. It was situated at the corner of Sunderland Street and Frederick Place, the entrance to the 'Lake' fairground. Today, the modern Buff's Social Club stands on this site.

A RARE VIEW OF THE 'LAKE' at Houghton in 1882. The 'Lake' was created in 1881 by Joseph Coulson who had the area excavated and the nearby stream diverted. However, the lake was short-lived since mill owners downstream, being deprived of water-power, started legal proceedings for the restoration of the water supply. The lake was eventually filled in by showmen to form a fairground.

THE FESTIVAL OF HOUGHTON FEAST has been celebrated every October for over 800 years and people came in their thousands from far and wide, to enjoy the many attractions of the 'Feast'. This photograph shows the Lake fairground at Houghton Feast in around 1895.

HAMILTON'S ICE-CREAM STALL, inside the Sunderland Street entrance to the Lake fairground at the annual festival of Houghton Feast, in around 1905. Seen at the far left is Mr Wm. Hamilton, sen., with the small boy, George Wm. Hamilton, enjoying an ice-cream. Serving inside the stall are the Hamilton brothers.

A SHOWMAN'S CARAVAN with the family, at the Lake fairground during the festival of Houghton Feast in around 1912.

Sunderland Road, Houghton-le-Spring.

LOOKING UP SUNDERLAND STREET towards the 'Cut', around the year 1912. This once busy thoroughfare was completely demolished in the 1960s to make way for the reconstruction of the A690, Durham–Sunderland highway, that now cuts across the site of this street.

ANOTHER VIEW OF SUNDERLAND STREET, higher up the road in around 1900. On the extreme left is Hopper House, formerly the residence of George Hopper, ironfounder. The flat-topped building was for many years a branch store of the Hetton Downs Amicable Industrial (Co-operative) Society.

WILLIAM STREET was one of many that led from old Sunderland Street. Here the Wesleyan Church (see the photograph below) was situated, along with the old police station among other buildings. This photograph shows a police car in the police station yard in around 1925. At the controls is P.C. Nairns and sitting in the rear is Superintendent W. Lawson.

THE WESLEYAN CHURCH, WILLIAM STREET, is shown in this photograph of the 1930s. The church was erected in 1837 with the adjacent Wesleyan Schoolrooms being opened in 1851.

A VIEW OF HOUGHTON 'CUT' in the 1920s. At the right side of the photograph can be seen the lodge and entrance to the old hill-side cemetery, which was consecrated in 1854. At the time of the photograph the 'Cut' was very narrow and the road, the Durham–Sunderland highway, was very steep.

A MUCH EARLIER VIEW of Houghton 'Cut' in the year 1891. Hewn through the limestone rock in early times, improvement work on the 'Cut' was done as relief work by unemployed local soldiers discharged after the Napoleonic Wars. The 'Cut' was further improved in 1936–1938 and again in the late 1960s when the modern A690 dual carriageway was constructed.

CHURCH STREET, looking east from Broadway crossroads in around 1920. On the right, the Red Lion Inn and the parcel office of the Sunderland District Tramways Ltd.

AN OLD VIEW OF UPPER CHURCH STREET in around 1895. On the left, the raised footpath known as the Quay and on the far right the former Church Institute. Visible in the background is Houghton Hall, now the YMCA headquarters.

HOUGHTON RACES, held at the race-course, Hall Lane, was one of the many attractions at Houghton Feast in pre-war days. The photograph features one of the races, at the last race-meeting ever to be held at Houghton, during Houghton Feast in October 1938. Following the Second World War the race-course was developed as a housing estate, known today as the Race-course Estate.

A JUVENILE JAZZ BAND marching proudly from the Market Place, through Nesham Place, at a pre-war summer carnival.

HOUGHTON MARKET PLACE, looking west towards Houghton in around 1910. This is the site of the original village which had a large green and a freshwater stream which, by that date, had been enclosed.

UNTIL MODERN TIMES there were many small farms in and around the town of Houghton. One such farm – now demolished – was White-house Farm, situated near the Copt Hill Inn. The photograph shows the farm buildings in around 1895.

THE COPT HILL INN with a group of regular customers in around 1930. This interesting old inn seems to have originated as an eighteenth-century farmhouse. It became an inn in the early days of the Hetton Colliery Railway – opened 1822, closed 1959 – which crossed the road near to the inn front.

A VIEW OF THE COPT HILL RAIL CROSSING, looking west towards Houghton in around 1950, where the Hetton Colliery Railway crossed the Houghton–Seaham road. The Copt Hill Inn, subject of the previous photograph, stands nearby, to the right of this scene.

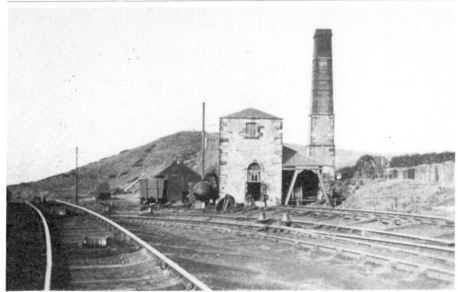

THE HIGH GROUND OF WARDEN LAW is situated two miles to the east of Houghton-le-Spring and it was here that the Hetton Colliery Railway reached its highest point. The photograph shows the steam hauling engine and transfer sidings in the 1930s. In the background is Warden Law summit, then the highest point of the area, but now much reduced in height by quarrying.

DIGGING OUT THE RAILWAY TRACK at Warden Law, following the great snow storm in February 1941.

THE BONFIRE ON WARDEN LAW SUMMIT, built by Houghton Boy Scouts for the celebration of the Silver Jubilee of King George V, May 1935.

THE ROMAN CATHOLIC CHURCH, Durham Road, in around 1905. Designed by the notable north country architect Ignatius Bonomi, the church was opened in November 1837.

WINTER TIME ON DURHAM ROAD in around 1910. In the background to the left is the Roman Catholic Church and School.

DURHAM ROAD AT RAINTON BRIDGE in the 1950s, looking south. In the foreground, Rainton Bridge spans the Rainton Burn while, in the background, Rainton Bridge crossroads can be seen and the railway bridge of the Moorsley–Lambton mineral railway.

WHITEHEAD'S GENERAL DEALERS SHOP – formerly the Plough Inn – at Rainton Bridge crossroads in around 1930. This site is now part of the Rainton Bridge traffic roundabout.

RAINTON BRIDGE over the Rainton Burn, in around 1895, with the Mill Inn in the background.

Dormitory 2   Redcar Camp, 1937.

SCHOOLBOYS OF THE HOUGHTON INTERMEDIATE (LATER BERNARD GILPIN), HALL LANE SCHOOL at the summer camp, Marske-by-the-Sea, Redcar, 1937. Teachers at the middle of the second row are: in the centre, the Camp Superintendent, to his left Mr Oliver and to the right Mr Gammie.

HOUGHTON URBAN DISTRICT COUNCIL, councillors and officers at Scruton House, Newbottle Street, 1936. Back row: (Ald.) H. Hodgson, Francombe, T. Newton, Metcalf, T. Coxon. Third row: J. Moran, Stevens, J. Hughes, (Ald.) M. Doyle, S. Warwick, V.J. Hunter, T. Richardson, J. Campbell. Second row: H. Calvert, Mrs Hodgson, Mrs Campbell, E. Earle, J. Hall (Chairman), Dorman, T. Coughlin, Dr W. Barkes, T. Wilson. Front row: Miss M. Oliver, Miss M. Laws, J. Robinson, Blenkinsop.

MR JONATHAN (JONTY) O'SHAUGHNESSY, proudly sitting on the saddle of his new motor cycle in around 1912.

MEMBERS OF THE HOUGHTON CYCLE CLUB enjoying the countryside near Finchale Abbey in around 1895.

SECTION TWO

Hetton-le-Hole

CHURCH ROAD, EPPLETON, with Nurse's Shop at the left in around 1918.

THE PARISH CHURCH OF ALL SAINTS, Eppleton, in around 1905. The ecclesiastical parish of Eppleton was formed in 1883, but the church of All Saints was not completed and consecrated until 1887.

EPPLETON CRICKET TEAM in 1935. Extreme left: Revd G. Salisbury. Extreme right: Linton Hope (scorer). Front row: second from left Revd Laws, fourth from left Mr Scott-Owen.

EPPLETON COLLIERY in around 1920. The colliery was completed in 1833 and by the 1920s employed 1,800 men and boys.

MINERS AT EPPLETON COLLIERY in around 1920.

A GROUP OF MECHANICS at Eppleton Colliery in around 1930.

AN EARLY VIEW OF CAROLINE STREET from the railway crossing in around 1905. On the left of the photograph is the Caroline Inn, still in business today.

MARKET STREET, from Caroline Street, in the 1920s. Then a busy shopping thoroughfare with a good variety of shops.

MURPHY'S FISH AND CHIP SHOP in Market Street in around 1930.

MARKET STREET FROM THE REGENT STREET END, in around 1920. At the right side of the picture are the premises of the Hetton Downs' Amicable Industrial Society.

MR GEORGE FISH, greengrocer and confectioner, standing in the doorway of his Market Street shop in the 1930s. The prices shown on the shop window are very interesting when compared with those of today, but at that time wages were also very low.

THE BUTCHER'S DEPARTMENT of the Hetton Downs' Amicable Industrial Society, Regent Street, in 1913.

HETTON AND DISTRICT WORKING MEN'S CLUB and grounds with bandstand and war memorial in the 1930s. In the background, to the left, Hetton Parish Church is visible.

LAYING GAS MAINS, alongside the track of the Hetton Colliery Railway, near to the Caroline Street level crossing in the 1930s.

THE WELL-STOCKED CART OF FRANK COX, hardware dealer, outside the Commercial Inn, Railway Street, in the 1930s. On the extreme left of the picture the doorway of the Union Street Methodist Church can be seen.

MEMBERS OF THE CHRISTIAN ENDEAVOUR, Union Street Methodist Church in 1958. Back row: J. Steel, J. Rennie, J. Rennie, E. Charlton, M. Craig, V. Ford. Middle row: J. Coxford, E. Potts, B. Gulliver, Revd F.W. Davies, I. Soulsby, T. Watson, M. Steel. Front row: P. Taylor, E. Cook, Mrs Davies, M. Tempest, B. McDonald.

BOYS AND OFFICERS OF THE BOYS' BRIGADE, Union Street Methodist Church, 1958.

CHILDREN AND TEACHERS OF HETTON INFANTS' SCHOOL in around 1905. The school at Front Street, Hetton, was opened in 1875. Following closure of the school the refurbished building was reopened as Hetton Branch Library in October 1961.

HETTON RAGTIME BAND, in around 1912.

HETTON BOG ROW GIRLS' SCHOOL opened in 1894 and was later enlarged. The photograph features pupils with a teacher in around 1918.

FRONT STREET, HETTON, near the Caroline Street junction, looking south in around 1910.

FRONT STREET, HETTON, looking north in around 1905. At the extreme left is the Barrington Boys' School, now Gateway supermarket. In the background can be seen the Infants' School, which is now Hetton Library.

THE ROUTE of the Sunderland and District electric tramway between Easington Lane and Grangetown – 1905 to 1925 – was laid as single track with passing-loops at half mile intervals. This photograph shows two trams travelling in opposite directions on a passing-loop at Front Street, Hetton.

AN EARLY CHARABANC at Front Street, Hetton, outside Humphry's optician's shop, with Hetton menfolk ready to set out on a day trip in around 1918. In the background to the right is the Hetton branch of Pittington Co-op Store, now Nutman's Fruiterer's shop.

THE HETTON BRANCH STORE of Pittington Amicable Industrial (Co-operative) Society at the corner of Front Street and Park View, in around 1914. Standing outside the shop in Park View is a Ford Model T Van.

PEACE CELEBRATIONS at Front Street, Hetton, in 1919. The official stand is set up in front of the premises now occupied by Nutman's fruiterer's.

PARK VIEW, looking west, following the great snow storm of February 1941.

A SUMMER FÊTE in the grounds of the disused Hetton Hall, in around 1912. The Hall, situated on a site near the present-day Leisure Centre and Swimming Baths, was formerly the property of the Bowes-Lyon-Barrington family and then, until 1865, it was the residence of Sir Nicholas Wood. The Hall was demolished in 1923.

A VIEW OF FRONT STREET, Hetton, looking south in around 1905.

Wesleyan Chapel, Hetton-le-Hole

THE MAIN ROAD AT HETTON, looking south, in around 1905. At the right of the photograph is the Wesleyan Church which was built in 1824 and behind, at the centre, part of Bleach Green can be seen. To the left, the old Conservative Club is visible.

THE PARISH CHURCH OF ST NICHOLAS, Front Street, Hetton in the 1930s. The original church on this site was erected in 1832 as a chapel of ease to Houghton. A new church was built on the same site between 1898 and 1901. This was consecrated by the Bishop of Durham on 29 April 1901.

WORKMEN AND WORKSHOPS OF JOSEPH G. WILLIS, timber merchant, agricultural implement manufacturer and coach builder, Office Place in around 1905. At the front centre, is a young Mr Nicholas Willis, father of Mr M.Willis, present owner of the firm of N. Willis and Sons, Motor Engineers, trading from these same premises today.

HETTON-LE-HOLE, St John's Ambulance Competition Team and Trophies, in 1939. Back row: J. Gilliland (Capt.), R. Hope, T. Duff, Supt. W. Stokoe, N. Wilkinson, N. Holmes, ? Widdowson. Front row: Mr Whitwood, Mr T.W. Stout.

IN EARLIER TIMES the community of Hetton was served by Hetton Station and the Durham (Elvet)–Murton–Sunderland railway which opened in 1836. This view shows the station and the Station Road bridge in around 1902. The railway closed in 1953 and part of the route is now a public walkway.

A VIEW OF STATION ROAD, looking south in around 1910. The larger building at the right is the former police station. In the centre background a tramcar can be seen.

HETTON POLICE SECTION at Hetton Police Station in around 1925. Back row: cons. Redding, Blackburn, Wilkinson, Pearson, Miller, Blake. Front row: cons. Taylor, Dryden, Sgt. T.H. Fowler, cons. Embleton, Redshaw.

STATION ROAD, looking north in around 1910.

MEMBERS OF HETTON LYONS COLLIERY MINERS' LODGE, with the Lodge Banner at the Durham Miners' Gala in 1932.

HETTON LYONS COLLIERY in around 1912. The colliery opened in 1822 and finally closed in 1950.

THE RAILWAY WAGON WEIGHBRIDGE at Hetton Lyons Colliery sidings in around 1920.

ONE OF THE ORIGINAL HETTON COLLIERY RAILWAY LOCOMOTIVES built by George Stephenson in 1822. Photographed in around 1880.

THIS SURVIVING STEPHENSON LOCOMOTIVE OF 1822, photographed at the Hetton Railway workshops after restoration in 1925, had for some years previously been used as a stationary engine to drive a sawmill. Later it headed the procession at the 1925 centenary celebrations of the opening of the Stockton and Darlington Railway and now is preserved at Beamish Open Air Museum.

MRS SHEPPERD at the doorway of her home at Wood Cottages, Hetton Lyons, in the 1930s.

WORKMEN AT THE HETTON WAGON-WORKS of the Hetton Colliery Railway in around 1920.

THE MAIN HETTON–EASINGTON LANE ROAD, from the Four Lane Ends, in around 1900. At the far right of the photograph is the New Inn, which still stands, while further along the same side of the street is the Abyssinia Hotel. The low cottages at the left were later replaced by Wakefield's grocery and provision stores. Today, the site is occupied by Moor House, home for the elderly.

THE PREMISES AND STAFF of William Wakefield Ltd, Grocers and Provision Merchants, at Four Lane Ends, Hetton, in around 1910.

THE ABYSSINIA HOTEL, near the New Inn, Four Lane Ends, in around 1920. Most of the area was redeveloped in recent times and modern houses now stand on this site.

Easington Lane and Moorsley

THE BOTTOM OF PEMBERTON'S BANK, Easington Lane, looking towards Four Lane Ends in around 1910. Prominent in this photograph are the single track and the trolley-wire standards of the electric tramway. On the left is Smith's Terrace with a group of ladies and children standing outside Watson's pawnshop. In the background, Lilywhite Terrace can be seen, with the shop of R. Lawson and sons, cabinet makers at the right.

PEMBERTON'S BANK looking towards Easington Lane in 1902. On the left is the shop of Miss C. Potts, draper and milliner. Some years later this same shop became the drapery department of T. Holmes and Sons. At the extreme right of the picture is part of the old Church Hall.

LOWER HIGH STREET, looking towards Pemberton's Bank in around 1910. On the right, between the buildings, the entrance to the churchyard of St Michael's Parish Church can be seen. In the foreground is the double track of a tramcar passing-loop.

THE FAMILY FIRM OF T. HOLMES AND SONS, grocery and provision merchants, was established at Easington Lane as early as 1866. The photograph features the premises of Holmes and Sons, at lower High Street, near to the gateway of St Michael's churchyard in around 1930.

THE BUTCHER'S SHOP of F. Westwick, situated at lower High Street, in around 1930. Standing in the shop doorway, holding a silver cup, is Mrs E. Westwick and on the left is her son, Mr F. Westwick. The decorated shop and window display promoting British Empire products was part of a decorated shop competition in Easington Lane Carnival.

EASINGTON LANE HIGH STREET, looking south in around 1900.

ANOTHER LONG ESTABLISHED BUSINESS at Easington Lane was the firm of J.G. Pringle, well-known for supplying quality groceries, provisions, drapery and footwear. The photograph shows a Pringle's delivery cart outside Pringle's Stores, at the corner of High Street and Murton Lane in around 1920.

MURTON LANE, looking towards Murton in around 1905.

BRICKGARTH, looking west from High Street in around 1920. Near the centre of the photograph is the Primitive Methodist church of 1869, which has now been replaced by a modern Methodist church. At the extreme right is the earlier Methodist chapel, dating from 1827.

A VIEW OF HIGH STREET, looking north in around 1923. On the left the village school of 1859 with its clock tower war memorial can be seen. Standing near the 'clock' at the tram terminus is a Sunderland District tramcar.

EASINGTON LANE CHURCH HALL AND CLOCK TOWER WAR MEMORIAL in the 1930s. The church hall was originally built as a school for boys and girls in 1859 by the Hetton Coal Company. The clock-tower was erected as a war memorial in 1920.

BOYS OF EASINGTON LANE SCHOOL in 1925. The school building, also the subject of the previous photograph, closed in the late 1920s. Pupils were then transferred to the Council School which opened in 1928.

EASINGTON LANE COUNCIL SCHOOL, football team and teachers with their many trophies of the 1935–1936 season.

THE TOP OF HIGH STREET, looking back towards Easington Lane in around 1905.

ELEMORE LANE, looking towards High Street in around 1905. On the left of the photograph is the Infants' School built in 1873. In more recent times the building was used as a Roman Catholic School.

A VIEW OF ELEMORE VALE, looking towards Easington Lane in around 1905. The group of children at the centre are standing near the Three Tuns Inn, now renamed 'The Vale'.

ELEMORE COLLIERY, showing the screening arrangements in around 1912. The colliery opened in 1827 and closed in 1974.

YOUNG UNDERGROUND WORKERS, at Elemore Colliery in around 1918.

THE MAIN ROAD AT LOW MOORSLEY, looking uphill towards High Moorsley in around 1910. At the extreme left of the photograph are buildings of Front Street, while at the right is Moorsley (North Hetton) Colliery which opened in 1825 and closed in 1915.

MINERS AT MOORSLEY COLLIERY in around 1895.

THE TEAM AND OFFICIALS OF MOORSLEY FOOTBALL CLUB, 1928–29 season.

CHILDREN OF LOW MOORSLEY VILLAGE SCHOOL in around 1905. The school was built in 1871 by the North Hetton Coal Company, and was for boys, girls and infants.

MEMBERS of The Moorsley and District Working Men's Club and Institute outside the club premises in around 1920. Back row: third from left, Mr B. Kirtley; seventh from left, Mr W. Ayre; eighth from left, Mr Williamson. Front row: Mr Baxter; Mr Cowley; Mr R. Brown; Mr Bell, Colliery Agent; Mr J. Howe; Mr J. Scott; Mr Prest; Mr Galley.

VILLAGERS OF MOORSLEY in front of the bonfire at High Moorsley, during the Peace Celebrations of 19 July 1919.

East, Middle and West Rainton

EAST RAINTON VILLAGE GREEN, in the 1920s. The higher building on the right of the photograph is the old Village Tavern, now a dwelling house, while on the left is the Wesleyan Chapel, founded in 1823 and rebuilt in 1889.

EAST RAINTON VILLAGE, looking north-west across the village green in 1960. Part of the Wesleyan Chapel can be seen at the right of the photograph.

NORTH STREET, East Rainton, in 1960. At the left of the picture, 'The Folds', now replaced by modern houses bearing the same name. The Wesleyan Chapel is visible in the background at the right.

THE HAZARD COLLIERY at East Rainton was sunk in 1818 and closed in 1935. In this photograph of around 1920, miners at Hazard Colliery lamp cabin are waiting to go underground.

EAST RAINTON, Hazard Colliery Cricket Team outside the clubhouse in around 1910. Although the Hazard Colliery closed in the 1930s this long established cricket club continued to progress. In more recent years the name was changed to East Rainton Cricket Club.

MEMBERS OF THE EAST RAINTON WELCOME HOME FUND in 1918.

CHILDREN of the old East Rainton Infants' School in 1919.

THE OLD SUNDERLAND–DURHAM main road at Middle Rainton in 1960. On the right of the photograph is Front Street, which was demolished only a few years later to make way for the reconstruction of the A690 Sunderland–Durham highway.

THE COE FAMILY outside their small shop at Front Street, Middle Rainton, in the 1920s.

A VIEW OF WEST RAINTON VILLAGE with St Mary's Parish Church and Church Row, in around 1920. The church was built originally in 1825 as a chapel of ease to Houghton and was rebuilt in 1864. The tower and spire were added in 1877 and were the gift of Sir George Elliott. To the right of the church can be seen the roof of the old school.

A LATER VIEW OF THE VILLAGE of West Rainton with St Mary's Church to the left, fronted by Church Row. At the right of the picture part of North Street can be seen.

THE CONSECRATION OF THE NEW BURIAL GROUND at West Rainton, by the Bishop of Durham in 1940. Front, left to right: Revd R. Watson (Rural Dean); Revd S. Nye (Rector, West Rainton); A Diocesan Officer; the Right Revd Alwyn Williams (Bishop of Durham). Centre of background group, P. Ronan (Chairman, Parish Council).

WEST RAINTON VILLAGE, North Street, in around 1920.

THE OLD RAINTON WORKING MEN'S CLUB AND INSTITUTE, at West Rainton in the early 1900s. The club was founded in the former dwelling house known as Oak Tree House.

THE ROBIN INN in around 1900, which formerly stood at the side of Robin Lane (West Rainton–Hetton) near to West Rainton.

THE RAINTON GATE BRANCH of Pittington Amicable Industrial Society in around 1912.

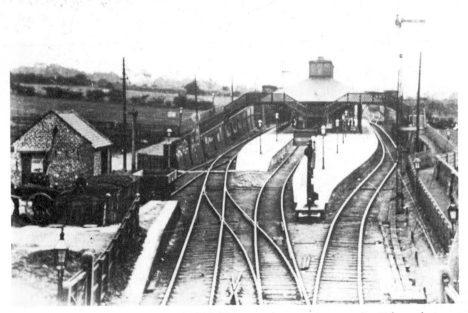

LEAMSIDE RAILWAY STATION in around 1910. This once busy station was situated on what was originally the main York–Newcastle route, until the Team Valley line opened in 1872. Since that time and until the early 1950s the station served the Sunderland–Durham local passenger services.

Chilton Moor, Fence Houses and new Lambton

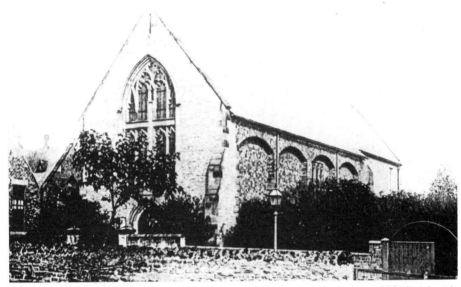

THE PARISH CHURCH OF ST ANDREW at Chilton Moor in around 1905. Built in 1876, the church was enlarged in around 1893.

CHILTON MOOR SCHOOL, adjacent to St Andrew's Church, was opened in 1872 and enlarged in 1886. The photograph shows children of the school with teachers, in around 1930.

THE BACK VIEW of the old cottages known as The Folds, at Chilton Moor in the 1920s. In the centre background above the pantile roof the top of the Londonderry Arms Inn can be seen. The area, now rebuilt, still bears the name The Folds.

THE CRICKET TEAM AND OFFICIALS of the Chilton Moor Cricket Club in 1938. Winners of the North-east Durham Cricket League, 1938.

THE 'LONG ROOM' CHILTON MOOR FARM, Black Boy Road, photographed in around 1970. Originally part of the early nineteenth-century Londonderry Collieries' workshop complex, it served as a military hospital during the First World War. The site of the recently demolished building is now occupied by houses of the modern Abingdon Grange Estate.

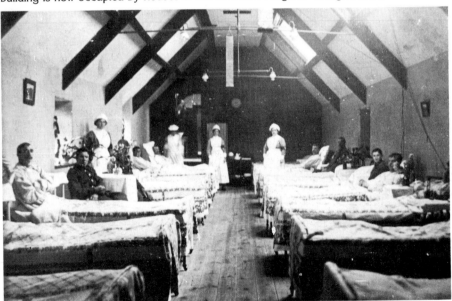

THE UPPER FLOOR OF THE 'LONG ROOM', the building featured in the previous photograph, when serving as a military hospital during the First World War. This picture was taken in around 1917.

DEMOLITION WORK IN PROGRESS at 'Long Row' Chilton Moor in the 1930s. The Londonderry Arms Inn can be seen in the background on the right. Avon Crescent now stands on this site.

DUBMIRE LADIES' FOOTBALL CLUB in around 1920.

A GENERAL VIEW OF THE MAIN ROAD AT BANKHEAD, looking south towards Chilton Moor, in around 1910. The main premises of George Graham Ltd, 'The People's Stores' are on the extreme left.

BLACKSMITHS AND HORSE-SHOERS of George Graham Ltd at the workshops, situated behind Front Street, in around 1910.

Bank Head, Fence Houses. 7075

A VIEW OF THE MAIN ROAD AT DUBMIRE, looking south-east towards Chilton Moor in around 1926. The group of shops on the left form the present-day Edinburgh Bakery while the building at the centre is the Wellington Inn. Passing the shops are a group of miners going to work in their working clothes, a common sight in the days before the introduction of pithead baths.

Station Avenue, Fence Houses. (765)

STATION AVENUE, looking towards Fence Houses railway station in around 1920. At the centre of the photograph is a tramcar of the Sunderland District Electric Tramways which has just departed from the station terminus.

FENCE HOUSES STATION, looking south, in around 1920. The station opened in around 1840 and was part of the main York–Newcastle route until the Team Valley line opened in 1872. In later years the station served the local Durham–Sunderland route, until passenger services closed in 1964.

A VIEW FROM FENCE HOUSES STATION, looking west in around 1920. On the left, Morton Crescent and on the right, the Fence Houses branch of Chester-le-Street Co-operative and Industrial Society.

NEW LAMBTON ROAD, with Lambton Cokeworks in the background, photographed in around 1970. At the left of the picture is the building of the former Lambton Swimming Baths and, at the right, the site of Lambton 'D' Colliery, which closed in 1964. Lambton Cokeworks closed in 1986.

A VIEW OF NEW LAMBTON in around 1905. The photograph shows rows of colliery houses, while behind them are the chimneys of the Lambton Brickworks and Cokeworks. At the far right is the Lambton 'D' Colliery.

WASHING DAY AT NEW LAMBTON in the 1920s. Gert Dawson in the back yard, 'possing' the clothes in soapy water inside the 'poss-tub'. Attached to the tub is an early type of wringer used to wring water from the washed clothes.

MILL ROW at New Lambton in around 1905. At the right is the railway embankment and bridge of the North Eastern Railway.

LAMBTON RAILWAY LOCOMOTIVE NUMBER 17 at Lambton Cokeworks, in around 1905.

BREAK NECK GILL at Fence Houses, looking west in around 1910. On the left is Morton Grange Terrace and, in the centre background, Gill Crescent.

LUMLEY SIXTH COLLIERY SILVER PRIZE BAND. Winners of 'Cassell's' Shield at Crystal Palace, 29 September 1928.

Bournmoor

BURNMOOR FROM SIXTH P

A VIEW FROM LUMLEY SIXTH PIT, looking north towards Burnmoor (Bournmoor) in around 1920, before housing estates encroached into the countryside. In the immediate foreground is part of Breckon Hill Dene and on the left Primrose Hill Cottages. In the background Burnmoor village can be seen with St Barnabas Church, the old Church Hall and the Village School, now the clubhouse of Burnmoor Cricket, Tennis and Football Clubs.

LUMLEY PARK DENE, better known as Breckon Hill Dene, was a favourite place for woodland walks and for children to play. The photograph of 1905 shows a group of boys enjoying a cool bathe in the stream.

PRIMROSE HILL COTTAGES in 1905, long before the surrounding area was developed as housing estates.

BURNMOOR VILLAGE SCHOOL FOR GIRLS AND BOYS was built in 1874 and enlarged in 1897. The photograph features a group of boys from the school with their teacher in around 1905.

BURNMOOR VILLAGE, then known as Wapping, looking west in around 1905. To the left of the photograph can be seen the Reading Rooms, while on the right is the row of cottages known as Long Row.

A DETAILED VIEW OF LONG ROW looking east in around 1910. Lambton Park Garden Centre now stands on this site.

BURNMOOR CRICKET CLUB FIRST TEAM AND OFFICIALS, 1932 season. Winners of the Horner Cup and the Echo Bowl. Back row: W. Rutherford (Hon. Sec.), T. Hardy, F. Woodhouse, C.L. Fairbairn (Capt.), J.L. Gelson (Vice Capt.), J.S. Blackbird, R. Yellowley, E.S. Clark, A.C. Lowerson (Hon. Treas.). Middle row: W. Brown, A. Weightman (Vice Pres.), M. Croudace (Pres.), J.R. Bond (Chairman). Revd A.J. Gadd (Vice Pres.), R.F. Forster. Front: T. Combey, A. Smith.

BIDDICK LODGE AT BIDDICK GILL, in around 1910. This attractive gateway formerly stood at the driveway entrance to Biddick Hall.

THE HAMLET OF HOUGHTON GATE in around 1905, with the Burnmoor road in the foreground and the Chester-le-Street road to the right. Houghton Gate was formerly the site of a toll-gate, one of several that existed in the Houghton area.

LUMLEY FORGE BRIDGE at Lumley Park Dene, better known as Breckon Hill Dene, looking north towards the hairpin bend and steep hill of Forge Lane, in around 1905.

A VIEW OF LUMLEY DENE and Breckon Hill village, looking south in around 1905, with Lumley Forge Bridge in the foreground. A concrete bridge of the A1(M) motorway now spans Lumley Dene at the location featured in this and the previous photograph.

Old and New Penshaw

OLD PENSHAW VILLAGE in around 1910. On the extreme left part of All Saints Parish Church is visible, while on the far right the Wesleyan chapel of 1778 can be seen.

ROSE STREET, Old Penshaw, in around 1912.

PENSHAW HILL AND PENSHAW MONUMENT in the 1920s. The monument, based on the Temple of Theseus in Athens, was erected in 1844 to the memory of John George Lambton, first Earl of Durham, statesman and first Governor General of Canada who died in 1840.

CHILDREN WITH THEIR TEACHERS at Penshaw Board School in around 1905.

THE RIVER WEAR AT BIDDICK, looking upstream towards the impressive Victoria Bridge in the 1920s. This large stone railway bridge, still in use today, is so called because the last stone was laid on the day of the coronation of Queen Victoria, 28 June 1838. Based on the Roman aqueduct at Alacantara in Spain, the bridge consists of four main arches, the largest having a span of 160ft, and three smaller arches at each end. Its total length is 811ft, while the height above high water level is 130ft. Visible here through one of the centre arches is North Biddick Colliery, and a small ferry boat carrying miners to the colliery can be seen crossing the river.

RIVER WEAR AND PENSHAW MONUMENT. FATFIELD. 798.

THE RIVER WEAR AT BIDDICK, looking down river in around 1910. On the extreme right is Penshaw Hill, with the monument visible on the skyline.

Fatfield Bridge.

THE RIVER WEAR with Penshaw road bridge, also known as Fatfield Bridge, in around 1920. This 155ft long iron bridge was opened in January 1890 by the third Earl of Durham.

NEW PENSHAW RAILWAY STATION in the 1920s. This station consisted of an island platform, with passenger access by means of a wide stairway that led from the main road on Penshaw bank.

COX GREEN STATION in around 1950. This rural station was on the Penshaw–Sunderland branch line which closed to passenger traffic in 1964.

SECTION EIGHT

Shiney Row

THE MAIN CHESTER-LE-STREET–SUNDERLAND ROAD at Front Street, Shiney Row, in around 1920. On the left stands Coffin Row, so called because of its shape, while at the right is Westbourne Terrace, now the main shopping precinct.

CHESTER ROAD AT SHINEY ROW, looking west in around 1910. On the left is the United Methodist Chapel, now the site of Trinity Church, while on the right stands Long Row, the site now occupied by Grangewood Close and Grangewood Garage.

HARRY LOW'S BARBER'S SHOP at Coffin Row in around 1910. Standing in the doorway is Harry Low with his small daughter Nina and assistant Joe Combey.

Quarry Head, Shiney Row. 3700

THE SHOULDER OF MUTTON INN at Shiney Row with a group of customers in the 1920s. At that time the main Chester-le-Street–Sunderland Road passed the front of the inn. At the extreme left of the photograph is Walter Willson's grocery shop. Beyond the Shoulder of Mutton can be seen Penshaw Place and the Wesleyan Chapel.

SHINEY ROW UNITED METHODIST CHURCH, Chester Road in around 1910. The main building was erected as a Wesleyan chapel in 1805, rebuilt in 1831 and demolished in 1956. On the right is the schoolroom of the 1890s, retained as part of the modern Trinity Methodist Church which was opened on 24 June 1972.

SHINEY ROW UNITED METHODIST CHURCH JUNIOR CHOIR with Choir Master Mr W. Hunter and pianist, Mr Alf Smith, in around 1930.

SHINEY ROW Primitive Methodist Church Football Team in around 1920. Back row: T. Dawson (Trainer), J. Porter, M. Smith, J. Stoves, J. Tulis, A. Chicken, W. Mace, J. Reed. Front row: ? Mace, J. Fletcher, A. Smith, R. Wilson, A. Middlemas.

TAYLOR'S FARMYARD was situated behind Westbourne Terrace with access by means of a wide passage way from the front street. The photograph shows Mr Taylor and his young son, Frank, with a calf in around 1930.

A HORSE-SHOER AT WORK, at Taylor's farm in around 1910.

A REFUSE COLLECTOR, with horse and cart at Prince's Street in around 1930.

SHINEY ROW COUNCIL SCHOOL was built in 1912 with separate departments for girls, boys and infants. The photograph shows a class of girls with their teachers at the school in 1920.

Herrington Burn and Philadelphia

A VIEW OF HERRINGTON BURN looking towards Shiney Row in around 1920. The tracks of the tramway system can be seen with the main line turning to the right towards Herrington and beyond. Standing on the track is a tramcar ready to depart for Penshaw railway station.

THE 'BURN' AT HERRINGTON BURN, viewed from the road bridge, looking east towards New Herrington in around 1905. In the centre background can be seen the old Rose and Crown Inn and Herrington Mill.

MILKING TIME at Herrington Burn Farm with the farmer's daughter, Miss Hunter, in around 1905.

SHOPS AT ALMA PLACE, Herrington Burn, in around 1910.

MEMBERS OF THE HERRINGTON BURN WELFARE COMMITTEE at the newly opened Colliery Welfare Hall at Herrington Burn in 1928. The Welfare Hall is on the left of the photograph, while in the background the Tivoli Cinema can be seen.

HERRINGTON BURN in the 1930s. On the right side of the photograph is the Tivoli Cinema and, in the centre, the Welfare Hall.

PHILADELPHIA POST OFFICE and general dealer's shop in around 1920. At the right of the picture is the old Lambton Castle Hotel, while on the far left Raglan Row can be seen.

A GROUP OF PHILADELPHIA MENFOLK, sitting in a charabanc, outside the Lambton Castle Hotel, before departing on a day trip in around 1920.

AN OLD VIEW OF PHILADELPHIA LEVEL-CROSSING in around 1902. At that time the houses in the background on both sides of the main road were single-storey miners' cottages, with the back doors facing the road.

THE LAMBTON RAILWAY was an extensive private system which linked the collieries of the Lambton, Hetton and Joicey Collieries Ltd with the riverside staithes at Sunderland. Locomotive No. 9 is seen here with its crew and other railwaymen at Philadelphia engine sheds in around 1920.

ALSO LOCATED AT PHILADELPHIA was the extensive Lambton Engine Works of the Lambton Collieries Company. This photograph shows a group of joiners and pattern-makers at the workshops in around 1925. In the foreground are examples of their workmanship; wood patterns for the iron-foundry.

THE MARGARET (PEGGY) COLLIERY at Philadelphia in around 1920. Originally sunk in 1757 the colliery closed in the 1920s. However, the shaft continued in use as a ventilation shaft to the Dorothea Colliery and later to New Herrington Colliery.

THE TRAMCAR SHEDS of the Sunderland and District Electric Tramway Company (1905–1925) were located at Philadelphia. These sheds are now a 'Northern' bus garage. This photograph of around 1918 shows a horse-drawn inspection tower used for inspecting the overhead electric tram wires.

LAMBTON ENGINE WORKS SPORTS CLUB AFC team and officials in 1938. Winners of Washington District Aged Miners' Cup 1937–1938 season. Officials: T. Tindle, G. Edger, ? Green, ? Twinn, F. McIntyre, J. Atkinson, F. Robson, M. Willis. Team, back row: J. Clark, J. Ord, F. Charlton, L. Maderson. Middle row: L. Rumney, R. Hall, W. Edger, R. Minto, B. Collinson. Front row: W. Robson, S. Green. B. Kirtley (Sec).

PHILADELPHIA CRICKET CLUB SECOND TEAM. Champions in the 1933 season. Back row: R. Freake, G. Thewlis, J. McCall, J. Ord, T. Greenshield. Front row: W. Barron, C.V. Dixon, F. Malcolm, S. Blackbird (Capt.), N. Lee, A. Wilson, H. Slawther.

SECTION TEN

New, West and Middle Herrington

MARKET CRESCENT, New Herrington, in around 1912.

THE MAIN ROAD AT NEW HERRINGTON, looking east in around 1905. On the left, Banks and Grieves Buildings, while at the far right is George Street, East. In the centre background Catherine Terrace can be seen.

GRIEVES BUILDINGS at New Herrington in around 1890. The proprietor of the shops, Mr Oliver, is standing by the horse on which his son is mounted.

FRONT STREET AND GRIEVES BUILDINGS, New Herrington, with Market Crescent in the background in around 1930.

GIRLS OF NEW HERRINGTON COUNCIL SCHOOL with their teacher in 1929.

NEW HERRINGTON WORKMEN'S CLUB BOWLING 'B' TEAM, winners of Club Union Bowls Tournament, 1921 season. Back row: D. Thompson (Groundsman), T. Grundy, J. McKinley, T. Slassor, T.D. Brown, G. Saxon, A. Escott, J. Frazer. Front row: E. Mitcheson, G. Burgen, R. Dawson, J. Scott, C. Stokoe (Pres.), J. Brown, J. Ingleby, W. Brown (Capt.).

NEW HERRINGTON WORKMEN'S CLUB MILITARY BAND. Photographed in front of the old club pavilion in 1908. At the front, centre, is the conductor, Mr Calvesbert. The band included several members of the Scott family. Back row: fourth from left, Mr T. Scott; tenth from left, Mr C.M. Scott. Second row: eighth from left, Mr T. Scott; ninth from left, Mr W. Dennis (Secretary). Front row: third from left, Mr W. Scott; fourth from left, Mr C. Scott.

A GROUP OF MEMBERS of New Herrington Workmen's Club, outside the club premises in around 1912.

NEW HERRINGTON COLLIERY, known locally as the 'New Pit', was opened in 1874. It was reconstructed in the early 1950s and closed in November 1985. The photograph shows the colliery surface arrangements in around 1912.

ST AIDAN'S PARISH CHURCH, New Herrington, in around 1910. The church was consecrated by the Bishop of Durham on 19 July 1886.

A VIEW OF WEST HERRINGTON VILLAGE in around 1905. On the left stands the old Manor House while at the right is St Cuthbert's Church. In the centre background the Shoulder of Mutton Inn can be seen with other buildings.

WEST HERRINGTON VILLAGE in around 1910. The Shoulder of Mutton Inn is on the left and on the right is the large house known as The Lodge.

MIDDLE HERRINGTON FARM AND CROW LANE, in around 1890.

CROW LANE AT MIDDLE HERRINGTON, in around 1890, with the old houses of Foxcover Lane in the background.

CROW LANE, MIDDLE HERRINGTON, looking west in the 1930s. On the left is the Middle Herrington Methodist Church.

Newbottle and Sunniside

SITUATED ON A HIGH RIDGE above the neighbouring mining communities, the village of Newbottle remained relatively unaffected by industrial development. This view of around 1908 shows a tramcar standing in front of the William IV Inn. At the left is Newbottle House, now Newbottle Workmen's Social Club, while in the background on the right St Matthew's Parish Church can be seen.

LOOKING UP SOUTH STREET in around 1912. In the background centre, the central premises of the Newbottle and District Co-operative Society can be seen.

MEMBERS OF THE BUTCHERING DEPARTMENT at the Newbottle premises of the Newbottle and District Co-operative Society in around 1920.

HOUGHTON ROAD, NEWBOTTLE, at the top of Newbottle Bank, looking towards Houghton in 1912. On the right, the Old Queen's Head Inn and in the background a tramcar is approaching the top of the Newbottle Bank.

GIRLS OF NEWBOTTLE COUNCIL SCHOOL in around 1920. The school opened as a local Board School in 1880 and was enlarged at a later date.

NEWBOTTLE ROVER SCOUTS in around 1930.

MR F. TINDALE, DAIRYMAN, with horse and milk-float at South Farm, Newbottle, in the 1920s.

FEEDING TIME AT WEST FARM, better known as Coulson's Farm, in 1912, where a young Miss Francis Lishman is feeding poultry in the farmyard.

GATHERING THE HARVEST with a self-binding reaping machine at 'Over-the-Hill Farm' near Newbottle in 1918.

A FARMYARD SCENE NEAR NEWBOTTLE in around 1918. Here corn is being threshed by means of a steam-driven thresher, the threshing team being assisted by farm workers. After the harvest, during the autumn, the threshing outfit moved from farm to farm.

THE MINING HAMLET OF SUNNISIDE, between Newbottle and Houghton, consisted of three long rows of colliery houses and a Methodist chapel. This photograph shows McArdle's general dealer's shop at the top of South Row in the 1930s.

SUNNISIDE METHODIST CHAPEL was the centre of religious and social life in this mining community. Supporting, among other activities, its own football team, choir and brass band. This photograph features the Sunniside Chapel brass band outside the chapel premises, in around 1912.

BIBLIOGRAPHY

1. Fordyce, W. *History of the County Palatine of Durham*, 1856.
2. Hope, R. *Old Low Moorsley*, 1988.
3. Ronan, *P. West Rainton. A History* (Unpublished), 1988.
4. Smith, C.A. *Hetton-le-Hole. Official Guide*, 1960.
5. Smith, C.A. *Houghton-le-Spring. A Guide*, 1963.
6. Smith, C.A. *The Sunderland Echo*. A series of articles on Houghton, Hetton and District, 1960–1962.
7. Whellan, F. *History of the County of Durham*, 1894.
8. *Hetton. The Development of a Community*, Hetton Community Association, 1973.
9. *Hetton-le-Hole. Official Guide*, 1930.
10. *Houghton-le-Spring. A Guide and History*, 1923.
11. *Kelly's Directory of Durham*. Various Dates.

ACKNOWLEDGEMENTS

Most of the photographs included in this book have been drawn from the author's collection, built up over the years with the kind and generous help of many people. Sincere thanks are extended to all those who have, in years past or more recently, given or allowed to be copied their postcards and photographs; or have supplied invaluable information.

Acknowledgement for kind permission to publish photographs is also due to:

The Revd P. Fisher, Rector of Houghton-le-Spring ● The Hetton Methodist Church ● The late Philip Ronan ● The K. Taylor Collection ● The Sunderland Echo ●Beamish, North of England Open Air Museum.

Finally, special thanks are given to Marion Moore and Derrick Richardson for help with the text and preparation of the typescript.